For the Souls with Different Tones

DEDICATION

To my parents, who persistently
inspires to achieve my goals. To every
person of color in society who faces
struggles in society daily due to
their cultural background.

ACKNOWLEDGEMENTS

Two individuals in my life
have contributed greatly to the
production of this piece. I extend
my deepest gratitude to Mr. K. Odlum
and Ms. C. Christopherson for setting time
in their schedule to revise and provide
feedback on my drafts.

PREFACE

Racial inequality has been a prevalent issue for decades. It divides our society in ways that defeats the concept of cooperation. Racism affects everyone. But youth of color are impacted by racism the most. Race is a factor that is often used to determine the punishment of a young person. The mental health of youth of color is also impacted negatively due to the exposure of racism. The presence of racial inequality in the education system and the workplace places a damper on the success rate of youth of color. The main method that can be used to lessen the harm of racism on youth of color is education. This can be done through the influence of adult figures, (ex: parents and teachers) who can aid youth of color in becoming more aware of issues surrounding race.

TABLE OF CONTENTS

BOOK ONE: UNJUST PUNISHMENT

<u>CHAPTER ONE</u>

Today starts off as an ordinary Monday. Like every other morning, I reluctantly wake up at five thirty, prepare for school, and am out of the house by six fifteen. I pull into the school parking lot after twenty minutes of dreadful morning commuter traffic. School does not start for another half hour, so I have a moment to collect myself. After a couple minutes, I decide to get out of my car to take on the day. The moment my foot touches the dark gray pavement of the parking lot, my best friend, Rayanne ambushes me.

"Good morning Dulanda!" she exclaims, with her hazel eyes bulging from her head.

"Hey Rayanne – looks like you are having a spectacular morning!" I reply, with a sly grin.

"Today is such a beautiful day! Look around – the sky is blue, the trees are flourishing, the birds are chirping! It is simply magical," she says in awe.

I look down at my phone to check the time. There are officially twenty-five minutes until the first bell rings. Rayanne and

I share all our classes together, so I grab her hand and we walk into the building to start another uneventful week of learning (or at least I think it will be).

###

Rayanne and I walk into school to hear yelling and screaming. We rush to the Commons to see what the hoopla is about. As soon as we reach the Commons we see a large group of students surrounding something. Since we are both short, we can't see anything. I tap on a nearby upperclassman to figure out what's going on.

"Some black freshman is fighting with a white freshman because he [the white freshman] was saying blatantly racist things to him."

The upperclassman moves to the side to let me get a look of the fight. My eyes cannot believe what they are seeing. The "black freshman" is my younger brother, Dion. My older sister instincts force me to break through the crowd. Once I get through the large mass of students who are recording and encouraging the fight, I try to get in between Dion and the other freshman. But I am too late. The student resources officer and school principal Mr. Johnson storm through the crowd and goes in between the two boys. The officer then turns around, detains Dion, and removes him from the scene. The "white freshman", whose name is Lawrence, leaves with the principal. I run after the officer as he places Dion into a squad car at the front of the school.

"Wait! Where are you taking him? Stop! I am his sister!"

"To the juvenile detention center. North Primavera has a zero-tolerance policy for fighting."

2

CHAPTER TWO

I reenter the school and head to Mr. Johnson's office, in need of answers. I knock on the door and wait until he grants me permission to come in. I walk into the office to see Mr. Johnson sitting at his desk and Lawrence on the other side. I try not to glare at Lawrence.

"Good morning, Mr. Johnson. I am Dulanda, the older sister of Dion. Why is Dion heading to the juvenile detention center, and Lawrence is sitting here? I understand the school has a zero-tolerance policy for fighting, but why is Dion's punishment so extreme?"

"Well Dulanda, Dion resorting to violence poses as a threat to the school. It is my and the officer's job to protect the faculty and students."

"There are other methods of punishment available that are less cruel. Also, Lawrence's racist remarks is a threat to African American students and faculty in this school. It's bullying. His "speech" incites violence."

"Look Dulanda, I do not have time to argue with you. You do not have time either – your classes are about to begin soon. What's done is done. Please go to your class."

I obey his command and head to my first class. Lawrence snickers as the door shuts behind me, but I pay him no mind. This is not over.

###

I arrive at my class only to receive a message from the office saying my parents want me to come home. I drive home both calmly and frantically. Once I step through the door the sound of my mother sobbing in the living room greets me. My father and younger brother are comforting her as she lies on the couch.

"I want Dion to come home! Dear Lord, send him home!" she screams in between sobs.

I go over to my family and give them each a hug. It breaks my heart to see them like this. But I must remain strong. I must fight for Dion, and other African American students who receive unfair punishment in the public-school system. I head to my room to devise a plan – a plan that will bring a large amount of attention to the issue. That's when a lightbulb in my mind turns on - I should organize a protest! I grab my phone to text Rayanne about my idea and she replies showing great support. Once school is over for the day she comes over to spend several hours planning the protest. It will take place at the end of the week, at the front of the school. Students will gather with signs and chant for justice for Dion in a peaceful manner. I will even be giving a speech in response to the great injustice. After working out the kinks a little further Rayanne and I proceed to endorse the protest via social media. While

4

uploading photos of a flier for the protest, I receive a phone call from an unknown number, but a very familiar voice.

"Dulanda, it's me, Dion. I'm scared. I want to come home. What are they going to do to me?

"They aren't going to do anything to you, Dion. I promise. Just lay low, follow directions, and do not talk back. You will be out of there soon. I will fight for you."

CHAPTER THREE

The day of the protest sneaks up on me quickly. Feelings of both uncertainty and excitement are flowing through my veins as I enter the school, waiting for third lunch to occur. I frequently check my phone nonstop to see if there is information on Dion's status in the detention center. There isn't any. I meet up with Rayanne in the library, who appears to be as enthusiastic as I am, before the first bell of the day rings.

"Hey Dulanda – ready to seek justice and reform? What if the protest makes us go viral? We could be famous! That'd be epic!"

I laugh and flash her my signature sly smile. Nothing can put a damper on our day.

###

Rayanne and I leave our second block class early to set up for the protest. Once we get to the front of the school we feel a great amount of astonishment. We go out to find a medium size group of students sitting outside, with signs that say JUSTICE FOR DION and PUNISH RACISM in bold letters. A podium stands next to them. I stand behind the podium and Rayanne takes a moment to teach the crowd a series of chants. Then we were ready. Rayanne officially begins the protest by calling out a chant, with the protesters and I joining her. Students passing through the hallway inside the school stop to observe and film. As the protesters continue to yell the chants I begin to give my speech.

"Good afternoon and thank you all for attending this protest. We are here today because my younger brother, Dion, is receiving unfair punishment due to his reaction to another student spewing words of hate. I strongly believe there is great inconsistency in our disciplinary system at not only this school, but in the county in general. African American students are frequently receiving extreme penalties for violating rules, while there are Caucasian students who violate rules and do not receive any disciplinary action. How and why is this acceptable? Things must change, not only for Dion but for other African American students."

Before I utter another word, I feel two taps on my shoulder. I turn to see Mr. Johnson, with a somewhat stern look on his face.

"Dulanda, please come to my office right now."

CHAPTER FOUR

I awkwardly enter the office with Mr. Johnson. He points to a chair on the other side of his desk as he takes a seat, motioning me to sit down.

"You already know what we are here to discuss. I want you to know that I have been thinking a lot about this situation with your brother. After reading complaints from various students, and most importantly your speech, I now realize my punishment for Dion is too extreme, and that it is unfair that Lawrence did not also receive discipline. Lawrence's remarks are hateful and offensive, going against the school's beliefs. As I result, I am revoking Dion's current punishment, giving him a less cruel one, and at the same time punishing Lawrence to a degree equal to Dion. I deeply apologize to you and your family for my ignorance in handling this situation. My job is to protect the students and faculty of this school, and treat them all equally, not create tension. Dion should be home by this afternoon – once again, I apologize."

I thank Mr. Johnson and leave his office in great excitement. I run over to Rayanne, who is still outside to tell her and the other protesters the news.

"Oh, my goodness that's amazing Dulanda! I'm so happy for you and your family!"

The crowd responds by breaking out into an applause. Everyone then disbands after the final clap.

###

When I arrive at my house after school cheerful noise and music greets me. I walk into the dining room to see my family sitting around the table with a cake, Dion in the center. I go over to him and give him a hug, tears running down my face. My family is together again.

BOOK TWO: IMPACT ON MENTAL HEALTH

<u>CHAPTER ONE</u>

I walk through my local makeup store in search of new base products – foundation, concealer, and setting powder. The homecoming dance is approaching quickly, so I need to get my shopping done promptly. I search up and down each aisle of the store multiple times, unable to find a product that caters to my deep cinnamon skin. I decide to ask a nearby sales associate for assistance. She is a tall woman with bright green eyes, jet black hair, and a big smile.

"Excuse me, ma'am, can you match me to a foundation shade? I prefer a matte finish and I have combination skin."

"Of course! Right this way!"

She takes me over to a vanity station set up in the back of the store and places four different foundation bottles on the counter. None of them look even remotely close to my skin tone. The sales associate swatches each foundation on my cheek. My predictions are correct – each foundation is noticeably too light for me. I pick up the foundation bottles, which contain the word "light" in their shade name and turn over to the sales associate in dismay.

"Are these really the darkest shades you have throughout the entire store?" I ask, searching around frantically.

"Yes ma'am!" she replies enthusiastically. "Maybe you should try a skin bleaching method to even out your skin so you can match these! It would actually look prettier that way!"

Taking great offense, I jump from the chair in a hurry, not even bothering to thank her for her "service" and exit the store in disgust, wiping the foundation off my cheek. How dare she speak to me that way, and so calmly too? I get into my car and drive down the freeway, trying not to shed a tear over what has happened to me. Once I stop at a red light I glance into the car mirror at my skin in sadness. When the light turns green I proceed on my journey home.

#

I break down into tears when I reach my bedroom. I place my face into my pillow to drown the sounds of my misery. My breakdown lasts a good five minutes. I spend the rest of my afternoon wallowing in self-pity, cutting myself off from my family. My self-esteem is, I feel, in peril now, all because of an unnecessary remark toward my identity. I am not sure how this feeling will be resolved, if it ever is resolved.

<u>CHAPTER TWO</u>

My depressive episode lasts for quite a while. I feel apathetic towards everything – including playing with my dog. I am even planning on spending today isolated away in my room. But then I remember I have a hair appointment at the local hair salon as part as my preparation for homecoming. As a result, I reluctantly roll out of bed, slip on my cozy high-tops, and head out to my car to leave.

#

Traffic is light (for once) so I make it to the salon with a couple minutes to spare. I decide to stop at the coffee shop next door to get a cotton candy Frappuccino- my favorite drink. Once the barista hands me my drink, I swiftly towards the salon. When I walk in the strong smell of a straightening iron, shampoo, heat protectant sprays, and a friendly receptionist greets me.

"Good morning! How can I help you today? Do you have an appointment with a stylist?" the receptionist asks. She is average height, has a pixie cut with purple streaks, and a sleeve going down her right arm of various Shakespearean quotes and images.

I show her an email confirmation on my phone I have for an appointment with the master stylist, Lexis. The receptionist scans the barcode from the email and tells me to take a seat on a gray

12

couch until Lexis is ready for me. While I wait, I sip on my Frappuccino and scroll through my social medias. After a couple moments, Lexis calls me over to her chair. I'm taking a significant risk by going to an unfamiliar salon for an unforgettable event – anything can go wrong. But spontaneous activities are my cup of tea. Plus, her portfolio on her social media and reviews online are excellent. I have faith in Lexis's abilities.

"Hello Dulanda! I am Lexis – how are you?" Lexis is about five feet tall, dark silver hair, tan skin, and has mahogany brown eyes. She seems to be no older than thirty.

I remove my bonnet to reveal my fresh, tight, and black coils, and Lexis stares in awe. She runs her hands through my hair, trying to stretch it out. She then gives up and backs away in dismay.

"I am sorry, but I am not going to be able to do your hair. It is just too unkempt looking and would take way too much effort," Lexis says coldly, removing the cape she had draped over me.

As I stood from the salon chair, the other women in the salon getting their hair done are watching me, whispering to one another about what they had just witnessed. My cheeks are burning as if a dragon's breath hit my face. My hands begin to form fists at my sides. I slowly make my way to the door in embarrassment. As I pass the stylist chair closest to the reception desk I hear Lexis say something behind me in frustration.

"This is exactly why I do not like working on black people! Her hair is just too ugly! When will black girls like her learn that their hair looks better with a relaxer? I would hate to have that horrific texture."

The other women in the salon break out into laughter, and I run straight to my car in the busy parking lot.

CHAPTER THREE

I speed home and lock myself in my room, like when I came home from the makeup store. I collapse onto my bedroom floor, bawling like a restless infant. This is it for me. I am at my breaking point. I begin to hyperventilate uncontrollably and throw objects all over my room. I crawl into my bed, still in tears, and stare at my ceiling in complete silence. I take a moment to recall the events I have experienced the past few days. I wish there were people like me as part of society's standards of "perfect". Why do people not think I am beautiful? I wish I was enough for this world. I wish this feeling of despondency would leave my body. During my whirlwind of depressing thoughts there is a knock on my door. It is my mother.

"Dulanda, what on Earth is wrong? Is everything alright? Did something happen?"

I decide to relay to my mother everything, from the makeup store, hair salon, to now. Once I finish explaining my mother hugs me tightly.

"Oh, Dulanda. I'm so sorry – we live in a cruel world. You are beautiful – never forget that, please. Do not let the negativity get to you. You are a wonderful young woman, with a personality and future so bright. I thank God every day for you. Please keep your head up high – you are worth so much more than a couple hateful words."

I start to cry once again, feeling a bit better because of my mother. My eyes then slowly close and I fall asleep, while still in my mother's arms.

####

I spend the next couple weeks following my heart to heart moment with my mother to discover and better myself. I now attend weekly therapy with my mother and journal my thoughts daily. I also spend my days focusing more on the positive, rather than the negative. I realize that I owe it to myself to practice self-love often, or better yet daily, to ensure internal stability. Most importantly, I am extremely grateful to be going through this journey of restoration with my mother. I cannot imagine going through this alone.

BOOK THREE: PRESENCE IN WORKPLACE AND EDUCATION

CHAPTER ONE

Now that school is over with I have been looking for ways to keep myself busy this summer. I end up deciding to apply for a part time job at a trendy clothing store in the local mall. According to various sources, the benefits there are top-notch: above minimum wage pay rate, employee discount, flexible and manageable hours – it is everything I could want in a summer job. After completing lengthy research on the job offer and composing a well-written resume, I call the store's management department to set an interview date.

#

I walk into the store on the day of my interview with great confidence. I go to the nearest sales associate with a name tag that reads Zane for assistance.

"You are here for an interview? Oh, you must be Dulanda!" Zane states enthusiastically. He is tall, lean, nicely dressed, and has dark green eyes.

I nod my head and smile in reply. Zane then beckons me to follow him to an office in the back of the store with the word

"MANAGEMENT" printed on the door. He knocks on the door, waits for a response from the inside, and then opens the door to usher me in. At a desk inside the office is an older, blonde-haired woman with sharp blue eyes, wearing a dark gray pantsuit and dark navy pumps. I sit down in front of her and place my resume down calmly.

"Ah hello Dulanda, I am Mrs. Louis. I have been expecting you."

After speaking Mrs. Louis takes a few moments to stare at me inquisitively. Her eyes scan me closely from my hair to torso. I could feel my face burn in embarrassment. Mrs. Louis then takes my resume, holds it in her hands for a mere second, and proceeds to throw it into a shredder behind her. I am too furious to speak, so I watch in silence.

"I am sorry, but I do not think you have the qualifications to be an employee here. Thank you for your time," Mrs. Louis utters coldly.

Feeling great mortification, I rise from the chair and exit the office.

<u>CHAPTER TWO</u>

My heart is pounding as I walk down the hallway. What could have Mrs. Louis meant by "not having the qualifications"? Did I make a poor first impression? Why did she look at me the way she did? So many questions, but no answers. I bump into Zane from earlier as I make my way to the store's exit and he stares at me with somber eyes.

"Look Dulanda. I know I should have mentioned this to you earlier but there is something you must know about Mrs. Louis" he whispers regretfully.

He brings me over to a side wall. The wall displays photos of all twenty-nine employees, including Zane's.

"Take a look at each of these photos. Spot the most obvious difference between you and the other employees."

It does not take a rocket scientist to figure out what the main difference is. All the employees are Caucasian, and I am African American. I look over at Zane.

"Mrs. Louis doesn't like hiring African Americans, or people of color in general? Why?"

"I honestly don't know – some say it's because she is from the Deep South and still possesses racial hatred. It's terrible."

"Then why haven't you reported her? Why is she getting away with this?"

"I have tried to numerous times, and when I do it results in me being suspended. And I can't lose my job here – no other company offers great benefits for their employees. Plus Mrs. Louis is a veteran employee for this brand – she's been working here every day for the past 25 years. Headquarters love her. She has them wrapped around her finger – what she says, goes. But maybe as a "customer", you can report her."

I stare at Zane like he's the craziest man on earth. "If Headquarters doesn't believe you, then what makes you think they would believe me?" I say this as if I don't care about the situation, but I really do. But I also don't want to cause a ruckus. I don't want to draw attention to myself. I turn to give Zane the best of luck with the rest of his career and leave the store.

CHAPTER THREE

After what happened with Mrs. Louis during the interview, I ended up not having a job this summer. I am afraid of being rejected by another employer because of my race, so I think it is best for me to simply hang low and spend my summer days with friends. But unfortunately, all good things must come to an end – I go back to school tomorrow, and I am not really looking forward to it. Another long year of waking up early, taking notes, and testing – how fun. Hopefully the new school year also brings forth brand new opportunities and experiences.

#

I kick off my first class of junior year in Criminal Justice with Mr. Matthews. He is a short and middle-aged individual, with dark hair and a thick beard. He speaks in a deep Hispanic accent.

"Hello class - welcome to Criminal Justice. I am Mr. Matthews. Before we get started today, I would like to give each of you an assigned seat."

The class moans and groans in detestation. Mr. Matthews begins to point towards various seats in the room for each student to sit in. He then looks at me and points to a seat in the very back of the room, a place I am not very known for sitting. Once the last student takes their seat Mr. Matthews begins his discussion.

"I want to begin our first class by stimulating your minds. So, I have one question for you all – what is a damaging aspect of our justice system?"

The classroom is silent. I immediately raise my hand to share my input. Mr. Matthews notices my hand in the air but averts his eyes when our eyes meet. He instead changes the subject.

"Well, since absolutely no one has anything to contribute, open your textbooks to the first chapter and take notes on the reading until the end of class."

I find it quite peculiar of him to say that, considering he knows he saw my hand in the air. I decide to disregard it and begin my reading.

#

I go about the rest of my first day of school in great confidence, only to realize I left something very important in my Criminal Justice class – my cell phone. Right after my lunch period I rush back to the classroom. I slowly open the door to find Mr. Matthews talking on the phone, with his back facing the door. As I tip toe in I can hear what Mr. Matthews is saying.

"There is this one black girl in my first block that I already know I am not going to like. She sits in the back of the room, so I will not have to call on her during discussions. No matter how many times I tell counseling not to put people like her in my classes they still do anyway – it is so frustrating."

CHAPTER FOUR

I quickly dip from the room before Mr. Matthews notices I was in there. Luckily my phone was sitting on the edge of his desk so it did not take too long for me to locate it. I run down the empty hallway frantically, with a million thoughts racing through my mind. Mr. Matthews saying "people like her" causes me to recall the job interview from the summer. I strongly believe that Mr. Matthews shares the same opinion about "people like me" as Mrs. Louis does. The phone call makes it completely obvious – he refers to me as my race, instead of my name, purposely places me in the back of the room, and does not acknowledge my presence in class discussion. My cheeks start to burn, in embarrassment and uneasiness. I continue to run through the hallway, until I bump into Mrs. Williams, the amazing school counselor.

"Well hello there Dulanda! Where are you rushing to? You look like you just saw a ghost!"

I take a moment to catch my breath before speaking. Instead of beating around the bush, I decide to tell her everything – the job interview, Mr. Matthews – the whole nine yards.

"Wow – Dulanda that is terrible. I am sorry you experienced this. But you do realize that your right to have an equal opportunity for a job and education is protected under Affirmative Action – what Mrs. Louis and Mr. Matthews are doing is illegal," Mrs. Williams states solemnly. "No one can purposely keep you from being successful because of your race. You should report these incidents."

#

Following the conversation with Mrs. Williams in the hallway I decided to report the incidents at the interview and Criminal Justice class to the clothing store's headquarters and the school board. Both Mrs. Louis and Mr. Matthews have lost their positions, because both the headquarters and the school board condone racial discrimination. I am glad I live in a world where guidelines are set to prevent individuals' hatred for being the reason why I do not excel. It gives me and my fellow African Americans access to opportunities my Caucasian counterparts have, allowing us to have an equal chance at success.

BOOK FOUR: ADULT INFLUENCE

CHAPTER ONE

A nightly routine I participate in with my family is watching the news together. We watch every news story the reporters discuss, regardless of the content – political, economic, and global issues. My parents incorporate this activity as a form of "family bonding" to make my brothers and me become more aware of the good, the bad, and the ugly of the world. But tonight's news report is nothing like the others.

The moment my mother turns on the television to our national news station we see a frightening sight. The words "POLICE SHOOTS AND KILLS A BLACK TEEN" flashes at the bottom of the screen in bold, black letters. Various photos of a teenager with dark gray eyes, and a pleasant and warm smile comes on the screen. Two adults then appear on the screen, wearing shirts with the boy's face on them.

"I want my baby back! He does not deserve this! He never wished to inflict harm on anyone!" a woman wails during an interview with a reporter. Alongside her is a man who resembles the slain teenager, comforting her. One can easily determine they are the boy's parents.

The news proceeds to describe the tragic incident. The teenager's name is Alex Stone, a sophomore in high school. He was shot and killed by an officer because he [the officer] thought Stone was trespassing through a gated neighborhood and was allegedly being defiant. The "gated neighborhood" turns out to be where Stone lives, but the officer refused to believe him. Following the description is a disturbing video clip, recorded by the neighborhood's surveillance camera.

"Hey! What are you doing here? You do not belong here! Where are you coming from?"

"Sir, I live here – my house is the brick one down the block. I am walking home from basketball practice."

"There is no way a black person can live here. Tell me the truth right now!"

"Sir, I am telling the truth – I promise! Why is it so hard for you to believe me? You can even go and ask my parents!"

"Do not talk back to me! I am an officer! Who do you think you are? You are just some black kid!"

The video shifts to show the officer tackling Stone to the concrete ground. Stone tries to break away, but the officer continues to suppress him. My brothers and I immediately cover our eyes, afraid to watch what happens next. Seconds later the sound of gunshots rings out. My brothers and I flinch six times – once for each gunshot the officer makes. Alex lets out horrific cries out for help. My parents turn off the television immediately. My family and I cling onto each other in silence for a while, trying to understand what we saw. My parents then send my brothers and I up to our rooms for the remainder of the night.

CHAPTER TWO

I get in bed as soon as I reach my room, to try to fall asleep. But I cannot. Instead I toss and turn, replaying the video from the news in my mind nonstop. Alex's grieving mother also runs through my head. I do not know what to think about this. But I know one thing for sure – I am afraid. I am afraid that Alex's situation will happen to my brothers, my parents, or even me – and there will be nothing I can do about it. I begin to feel my anxiety heighten even more, along with a lump the size of a boulder forming in my throat. I try my best not to cry. Exhaustion begins to creep on me slowly. By the time a single tear slides down my face my eyelids close.

#

I go to school the next morning feeling awful, not only because of a lack of sleep, but because of Alex Stone's death. Stone's life is lost far too soon. Because of that tragic night he no longer has a chance to graduate, get married and start a family, or even celebrate retirement. His family must feel terrible. I walk into my first block and sink into my chair, placing my head on my desk until the bell rings. Once the bell rings, my teacher, Mr. O decides to start the day with a "public service announcement".

"Good morning everyone. I am sure most of you are aware of the Alex Stone incident. It is truly a shame that terrible things happen to innocent people because of a person's hatred. I hope that none of you ever must face what he did, especially those of you who, unfortunately, are more susceptible to being racially profiled. I want all of you to know that the world is not out to get you. Please do not live in fear – continue to grow, continue to prosper, because you all are going to be the ones who change the world so that no one will lose their life over who they are anymore. My generation's time is coming to an end. Now it is up to yours."

My class erupts into an applause, along with a standing ovation for Mr. O. There is not a dry eye in the room. I rise from my seat, feeling the weight of the world's racial tensions lifting from my young shoulders. I walk towards Mr. O and give him a sincere hug.

"Thank you for taking the time to acknowledge this issue – it means a lot to me. I walked into this room feeling terrified of the future. Now I will be leaving this room feeling hopeful - thank you."

"You are absolutely welcome, Dulanda. Your life matters."

CHAPTER THREE

I come home from school in a brighter mood, because of Mr. O. His declaration truly uplifts my spirits. I no longer feel the way I did this morning. I walk into my dining room to find my parents and brothers sitting at the table. I sit down and join them.

"Now that all three of you are home, we can talk. Your father and I just want to check in with you after last night." my mother says warmly.

"We hope you three do not think we let you all watch the news last night with malicious intentions. We did not do it to make you afraid. We did it because we feel you all need the exposure to reality – the reality of a young African American. No matter how many years it has been since the civil rights movement, some people still possess hatred towards our people," my father explains serenely.

"I want you three to please not give up on yourselves, even when it may seem the world does not want you to win the game of life. Each of you are blessed with wonderful traits. We are proud of

29

who you all have become – and we hope you all are too. Do not let situations like this get in the way of your path to success," my mother states.

We all gather for a family hug that is at least three minutes long. It is quite amazing how much the love and guidance from adults who care about my wellbeing can help shape my outlook on the world.

Bibliography

Baig, Mehroz. "Perpetuating Inequality in the Workplace." *The Huffington Post.* TheHuffingtonPost.com, 12 Feb. 2014. Web. https://www.huffingtonpost.com/mehroz-baig/perpetuating-inequality-i_b_4770143.html. 29 Nov. 2016.

Bonnie, Richard J. "Diversity and the Effects of Bias and Discrimination on Young Adults' Health and Well-Being." *Investing in the Health and Well-Being of Young Adults.*, U.S. National Library of Medicine, 27 Jan. 2015, www.ncbi.nlm.nih.gov/books/nbk284777/.

Davis, Johnathan, R. "Making a Difference: How Teachers can Positively Affect Racial Identity and Acceptance in America." *The Social Studies*, vol. 98, no. 5, 2007, pp. 209-214, *eLibrary*, http://explore-proquest-com.proxy.librarypoint.org/document/274851750?accountid=142.

Eddo-Lodge, Reni. "'Beauty Doesn't Just Come in Shade Pale' Why Representation Is Still a Problem in the Beauty Industry." *Stylist Magazine.* N.p., 07

July 2015. Web.
https://www.stylist.co.uk/beauty/beauty-doesnt-just-come-shade-pale-representing-ethnicity-diversity-industry-race/136332. 29 Nov. 2016.

Garcia, Jennifer Jee-Lyn, and Mienah Zulfacar Sharif. "Black Lives Matter: A Commentary on Racism and Public Health." *American Journal of Public Health.* American Public Health Association, Aug. 2015. Web. https://www.ncbi.nlm.nih.gov/pmc/articles/PMC4504294/. 09 Mar. 2017.

Gaskin, Ashley. "Race Socialization: Ways Parents Can Teach Their Children about Race." *Pardon Our Interruption.* American Psychological Association, Aug. 2015. Web. http://www.apa.org/pi/families/resources/newsletter/2015/08/racial-socialization.aspx. 14 Feb. 2017.

Glod, Maria. "Va. Man Gets 'My Name Back,' Real Freedom; Pardon in '82 Rape Case Comes Amid Calls for Justice Reform." *The Washington Post*, 22 Aug. 2002,

www.washingtonpost.com/archive/local/2002/08
/22/va-man-gets-pardon-and-my-name-
back/4b216c0e-bb4e-4d5d-a49f-
9cc263e5c874/?utm_term=.80a1d1c6b210

Hing, Julianne. "31 Million U.S. Kids Live in Poverty
Today As Racial Inequality Deepens."*Colorlines*.
N.p., 18 Apr. 2015. Web.
https://www.colorlines.com/articles/31-million-
us-kids-live-poverty-today-racial-inequality-
deepens.14 Feb. 2017.

Kareem Nittle, Nadra. "Depression Is A Serious Effect
of Racism on Children and Youth.
About.com News & Issues. N.p., 31 Aug. 2016.
Web. thoughtco.com/childhood-
depression-serious-effect-of-racism-2834777. 14
Feb. 2017.

Mink, Gwendolyn. "Affirmative Action." Houghton
Mifflin, Boston, 1998, *eLibrary,*
https://explore-quest-
com.proxy.librarypoint.org/document/197207068
5?accountid=142.

Mujic, Julie A. "Education Reform and the Failure to Fix
Inequality in America." *The Atlantic*. Atlantic

Media Company, 29 Oct. 2015. Web.
theatlantic.com/education/archive
/2015/10/education-solving-inequality/412729/.
20 Oct. 2016.

Na, Ling. "Children and Racism: The Long-Term Impact
on Health." *AboutKidsHealth.*
AboutKidsHealth, 8 Aug. 2012. Web.
aboutkidshealth.ca/En/News/NewsAndFeatures/
Pages/children-racism-long-term-impacts.aspx.
21 Sept. 2016.

"Racial Inequality in Youth Sentencing." *The Campaign
for the Fair Sentencing of Youth.*
N.p., n.d. Web. fairsentencingofyouth.org/the-
issue/advocacy-resource-bank/racial-inequality-
in-youth-sentencing/. 20 Oct. 2016.

Radio, WUNC, director. *Marvin Anderson: After
Innocence from WUNC/The Story. Youtube,*
WUNC Radio, 6 June 2013,
www.youtube.com/watch?v=ZjUUiLk6pXQ

Tomaskovic-devey, Donald, and Patricia Warren.
"Explaining and Eliminating Racial Profiling."
Contexts 2009, pp. 34. *SIRS Issues Researcher.*

Wihbey, John. "Racial Bias and News Media Reporting: New Research Trends." *Journalist's Resource*. N.p., 26 May 2015. Web. 29 Nov. 2016.

ABOUT THE AUTHOR

Dulanda Saintcyr is a young leader working
to achieve equality for all. She is a part of
her hometown's NAACP council, and her school district's
superintendent's
Equity, Diversity, and Opportunity Committee. She aspires to
establish a legacy for herself in her community.